Freedom
of
the
Pulpit

Freedom
of
the
Pulpit

Lee C. Moorehead

Abingdon Press
New York • *Nashville*

FREEDOM OF THE PULPIT

Library of Congress Catalog Card Number: 61-5558

SET UP, PRINTED, AND BOUND BY THE
PARTHENON PRESS, AT NASHVILLE,
TENNESSEE, UNITED STATES OF AMERICA

To my life partner,

BETTY,

Whose love has invested my ministry

with a holy freedom

Preface

THESE PAGES ARE WRITTEN OUT OF A DEEP LOVE FOR THE office of preaching. My family recalls that as a small child I play-acted the role of the preacher, rearranging the living-room furniture as my pulpit platform. Once I built my own pulpit out of an abandoned orange crate. For hours I monopolized the time of my family while I heartily pretended that I was preaching the gospel. Little did I know then of the awesome responsibilities and stern requirements of an adult preacher in the real world.

In the real world I have come to understand that the pulpit is no place for pretending. The office of preaching is, I believe, the highest vocational privilege which can be bestowed upon a mortal man. To me it is the freest of all professions. In fact, all of my life I have heard much said about the freedom of the pulpit. For the most part I have simply taken that freedom for granted. Only in these last few years, as I have endeavored to preach in a world of ever-deepening crisis, have I inquired into the nature of that freedom. My exploration has shown me that this freedom is far more complex and taxing than the simple, romantic view I entertained in the days of childhood play-acting.

7

Freedom of the Pulpit

Now that I understand that the possession of this freedom carries a high cost, my respect for it is the greater. I have reflected on the experiences which have awakened in me a profounder appreciation for the privilege of preaching. Certainly a more adult respect began during my years as a student at Boston University School of Theology. In this great "School of the Prophets" I was introduced to the excitements of a truly prophetic tradition. My respect for the office of preaching was forever heightened by the vital and brilliant instruction I received from my teacher of homiletics, F. Gerald Ensley, now one of the leading bishops of The Methodist Church.

Hence a reverence for the pulpit has prompted the writing of this book. I am grateful to the editors of the *Christian Century Pulpit* for their original publication of my article "How Free is the Pulpit?" and for their permission to enlarge upon that theme.

Contributing significantly to this writing were the kindly and thoughtful encouragements of two of America's ablest preachers and defenders of freedom: Harold A. Bosley, the distinguished minister of the First Methodist Church, Evanston, Illinois; and the late Halford E. Luccock.

Finally, this book could not have been written had I not known the blessed freedom of which I speak. This freedom has been supplied to me by the great laymen of Indianola Methodist Church, Columbus, Ohio, who, for over fifty years, have never wavered in their witness to the freedom of the pulpit.

LEE C. MOOREHEAD

Contents

Contents

Chapter I

The Crippling Effects of Acquiescence

SOMETIMES A PARTICULAR CHURCH IS SINGULARLY praised for its free pulpit. This praise plainly implies that it exceeds most other churches in this characteristic. Such a citation constitutes almost an invidious comparison. According to Protestant principles can there possibly be *any* church lacking this distinction? Are there Protestant pulpits which are *not* free? Is the Bill of Rights, as applicable to the pulpit as the public park, being violated in our churches?

In these terribly trying times we churchmen ought to take a closer look at the freedom of the pulpit. As in so many other things we are inclined to take it for granted. Just how free is the pulpit? As the preacher stands in his pulpit week after week is he truly free to preach the gospel as God gives him the light to understand it? If there are any shackles on his speaking we ought to be finding out what they are.

There is mounting evidence that the average pulpit is not free. It appears to me that the preacher's freedom is threatened both from within and from without. In these days of racial, political and economic turmoil powerful forces have made it plain that they do not want "issues"

11

dealt with in the pulpit. Many preachers know, for example, that they will be dismissed from their churches if they use their pulpits to speak for integration. Recently one large church discharged its highly respected minister because he had written an article for a national magazine advocating "creative contact" between whites and Negroes. Because this evoked the displeasure of some members of his congregation, a special commission was appointed to study the situation. Several months later, after first supporting the pastor, the commission issued this justification of his dismissal: "The commission feels that the voice of the pulpit should be the voice of the congregation." Instances of this kind could be repeated from many parts of the country. Not a few churches, then, have demanded that the voice of the preacher echo, not contradict, the voice of the congregation.

Early in 1960 a new attack was mounted against the Protestant clergy under the fire-power of some very old but still effective ammunition. The United States Air Force discovered that there had been inserted surreptitiously into its training manuals the familiar and discredited charges that the Protestant clergy was seriously infiltrated by communist influence, that the National Council of Churches was being used as a tool of Moscow, and the Revised Standard Version of the Bible was poisoned by the pens of Red translators. As a result of these renewed attacks a furor was raised on the floors of the United States Congress and in the councils of the churches. Though the Air Force speedily withdrew the manuals alleging subversion in the churches, thousands of well-meaning lay leaders expressed the view that "where there is so much smoke there must be some fire." Many ministers were deeply aggrieved by these imputations of disloyalty regarding their patriotism and profession. The impression persisted that behind these charges and doubts there was swelling a deep-seated distrust of the freedom of the pulpit. This distrust, it was felt by many, expressed an intense distaste for the enunciation of the gospel in terms of political, social, and economic realities.

It is quite simple, of course, to distinguish the threats to the freedom of the pulpit which arise from without. But freedom is never a simple matter and the freedom of the pulpit deserves a careful analysis. Occupants of the pulpit have through all ages found themselves in conflict with both their congregations and the larger community in which the church lives. But far more serious, though less accessible to discovery and diagnosis, are the threats to freedom from within. There is in fact much evidence that the precious freedom of the pulpit is being eroded by default and disuse. Make no mistake about it: preachers are being silenced with their own consent.

Living as they do in a materialistic society, preachers of the gospel are suffering from a pernicious inward disease which might be called "acquiescence." We have acquiesced in the spirit of our times. Here is a word we ought to understand. When we acquiesce to some demand, and so agree to it, we become relaxed and "at rest." This is what the original Latin word meant. The words "quiescent" and "quiet" are drawn from the same source. Instead of serving as divine doctors who detect and treat the maladies of the age, we have ourselves contracted the diseases. Despite all the attacks which have been launched against the freedom of the pulpit from without, it can never really be destroyed from without until the preacher, in his failure to exercise that freedom, allows it to die within himself. The effectiveness of free preachers is being seriously crippled by acquiescence. Several symptoms tell the story of this disease.

I

In the first place we preachers have allowed ourselves to be too deeply affected by an affluent society. Herein lies a tremendous irony: when I entered the ministry nearly twenty years ago the life of the preacher was stereotyped as the life of poverty. "Poorer than a church mouse" was a phrase vividly describing the parson's lot. But now that our profession has overcome much of its material poverty, we have "progressed" to the place where our moral and spiritual sensitivities are being frozen by affluence. Though it is true that many ministers are still kept financially en-slaved at a mere subsistence level, a great many "have never had it so good." Though many preachers are still woefully underpaid, they are increasingly receiving comfortable salaries. Most ministers now have very good cars, some have very fine cars, and not a few own two cars. The aver-age parsonage now is a veritable palace compared with the leaky shambles described by Hartzell Spence in his much read book, *One Foot in Heaven*. Nowadays the state of the parsonage can be a big issue in the appointment of a minister.

One of the obvious reasons for this increasing material well-being of the minister is the fact that the most flourish-ing churches are to be found in the prosperous suburbs where the minister has a bargaining point in demanding that his living and driving conditions be commensurate with the bounteous surroundings of his parishioners. Hence laymen, in the most prominent and powerful churches, are more inclined to treat their spiritual advisers to the advantages of "gracious living." As a result ministers, materially and socially, are accepted as participating members of the middle class. But acquiescing in all of this pleasant living, the preacher stammers awkwardly when it comes to articulating the nature of the gospel.

In a remarkable book, *Leaves From the Notebooks of a Tamed Cynic,* which records his shrewd and incisive observations made during his 1915-1928 pastorate in Detroit, Reinhold Niebuhr has much to say about the freedom of the pulpit. He was particularly pained by the frequent instances in which he noted a minister's message being muffled by the acceptance of material favors. He tells of an occasion when he was entertained in the luxurious home "of a very charming potentate of the local pulpit." He was taken to his meeting in a big limousine driven by a liveried chauffeur. His host explained that the car was a gift of the congregation. This situation drew from Niebuhr's critical mind the following notations:

It will be a long while before we can convince laymen of the spiritual implications in standards of living in a civilization which knows of no other way to give a man a sense of achievement than to let him advertise it by outward show. But ministers ought to know better. . . . Furthermore there is a moral peril in accepting the largess of men to whom you are trying to minister. It is not that they try to take conscious advantage of your sense of gratitude, but that such dependence upon their generosity creates a psychological hazard against honest presentation of the truth. . . . Most of these modern appurtenances are toys which appeal to childlike people. When we sacrifice the adventure of trying to maintain an inner moral integrity, we are bound to seek for compensating thrills and to find them in our mechanical toys.[1]

In still more modern terms a preacher may own a car with "power steering" and not possess in his preaching the power to steer the hearts and minds of his people out of the materialistic sands in which they are sunk. And considering other prestige symbols of our culture, it might be said that the preacher who lives in a "ranch-style" parsonage may find himself corralled in the pulpit. True greatness does not require outward show and mechanical toys. The free preacher "shall not live by bread alone but by every word that proceedeth out of the mouth of God."

II

A second symptom of this disease of "acquiescence" is to be seen in the fact that we preachers have tended to conform, not so much to the commands of Christ, as we have to the popular image desired by many people.

It is ironical, of course, that the American minister is currently enjoying a high level of prestige. Will Herberg in his essay on American religious sociology, *Protestant-Catholic-Jew,* reports that "there can be little doubt that the 'minister of God' ranks high, and is rising rapidly, in

[1] (Hamden, Conn.: Shoe String Press, Inc.), pp. 212, 213.

the American scale of prestige." It is to be suspected, how-ever, that this rising prestige is not based on the ministry's prophetic power. In the same essay Herberg finds little evidence of prophetic transcendence:

Aside from occasional pronouncements by a few theologians or theologically minded clergymen, religion in America seems to possess little capacity for rising above the relativities and ambiguities of the national consciousness and bringing to bear the judgment of God upon the nation and its ways.[2]

Perhaps ministers, exercising prudence in a prosperous age, have been more inclined to serve as "domestic chap-lains" than as prophets. Someone has suggested that the Protestant minister has been lately pictured in literature and films as a moralist primarily concerned with sustaining the *morale* of the middle class. Many members of the clergy have become, in the phrase of Arthur M. Schlesinger, Jr., "the bland leading the bland."

Is this the kind of preacher the laymen in our churches really want? Phyllis McGinley provides a verse-portrait of such a man:

The Rev. Dr. Harcourt, folks agree,
　　Nodding their heads in solid satisfaction,
Is just the man for this community.
　　Tall, young, urbane, but capable of action,
He pleases where he serves. He marshals out
　　The younger crowd, lacks trace of clerical unction,
Cheers the Kiwanis and the Eagle Scout,
　　Is popular at every public function.
And in the pulpit eloquently speaks

[2] (Garden City: Doubleday), p. 64.

17

On divers matters with both wit and clarity:
Art, Education, God, the Early Greeks,
   Psychiatry, Saint Paul, true Christian charity,
Vestry repairs that shortly must begin—
   All things but Sin. He seldom mentions Sin.[3]

But how free is the man who never mentions sin in the pulpit? Such a man may be quietly conforming to the image his congregation has of him, but at the same time he is crippled with acquiescence.

One of the giants of the American pulpit was Rabbi Stephen S. Wise. No one upheld the freedom of the pulpit more grandly than he. Prior to the opening of his famous Free Synagogue in New York City he made some searching comments about the pulpit. "Invertebrate amiability," he declared, "constitutes a check upon pulpit liberty— the unwillingness to give offense and pain even when these are unavoidable." With piercing accuracy he pointed to the perils of the ministry which persist to this day:

An over-pastorized congregation, like over-pasteurized milk, is likely to be safe, but likelier still to be ineffectual. I dwell upon the possibility of over-pastorization because of the not inconsiderable and, on the whole, increasing peril that the preacher in our day degenerate into a mere social appanage. Formerly, as was well said, the prophets were stoned or burned; now they are dined and coddled into silence,—because they are not prophets. The preacher must, at every cost, if he respect

[3] From *Stones from a Glass House* by Phyllis McGinley. Copyright 1946. by Phyllis McGinley. Originally printed in The New Yorker. Reprinted by permission of The Viking Press, Inc.

himself and honor his calling, avoid the danger of what Emerson calls "wards and pensioners of the so-called producing classes." [4]

Indeed the very popular notion of the minister as "pastor to the flock" may be used to devitalize his role as preacher and prophet. Perhaps unconsciously many laymen have formed an image of the preacher in which he can be "dined and coddled" into a state of "invertebrate amiability." But the preacher who conforms to this image cannot stand up in the pulpit for the simple reason that he has no backbone. He becomes, in the term of Horton Davies, less a minister of the gospel and more a master of ceremonies.

III

A third symptom of our "acquiescence" is our distorted view of the current wave of religious popularity and prosperity. We have really suffered from an illusion regarding its depth and scope. Though we ought to be grateful for even "the revival of the interest in religion," our effectiveness and forcefulness in the pulpit have been crippled by defective vision. We have mistaken the glitter for gold.

The disease of "acquiescence" is closely related to another stubborn human ailment, "rationalization." We have been so pleased by the apparent success of religion in a troubled world that we have leaped to false conclusions. We have seen it to be more genuine than it really is. Hence we have neglected the sterner requirements of the gospel while toning down our preaching. Seeing that the churches are crowded and that more people belong to churches than

[4] *Free Synagogue Pulpit*, Vol. 1, No. 2, Feb. 1908, p. 28.

ever before, and hearing more talk about religion than ever heard before, we have mistaken this for a golden age. But at the same time we have so anesthetized our critical faculties that our vision has been closed to the prophetic insights of our faith. In this state of ecclesiastical euphoria, preachers have surrendered the ancient privileges of the prophets. Our situation may not be too different from that set forth in a bit of dialogue from Samuel Beckett's much-discussed play, *Waiting for Godot:*

VLADIMIR: Your Worship wishes to assert his prerogatives?
ESTRAGON: We've no rights any more?
VLADIMIR: You'd make me laugh if it wasn't prohibited.
ESTRAGON: We've lost our rights?
VLADIMIR: *(distinctly)* We got rid of them.[5]

We who preach in the name of Christ ought to remember his own response to his growing popularity. The Gospel of Luke reports his response most trenchantly: "When the crowds were increasing, he began to say: 'This generation is an evil generation; it seeks a sign, but no sign shall be given it except the sign of Jonah' " (Luke 11:29) . In a time of growing popularity Jesus did not surrender his right to prophetic insight. He was not flattered and his critical intelligence did not falter. He was not blinded by the glittering response. This is an important warning for preachers of our generation. In an age of religious prosperity we need to be keenly aware of what is happening. It is the propensity of the great prophet that at the very moment his influence increases he becomes more specific and definite in the preaching of the gospel. He will not get rid of his right to be a prophet as though it were a "hot potato."

It may be shattering to our present pleasure in the religious revival, but we who are committed to preach in the name of Christ ought to hear another of his warnings: "Woe to you, when all men speak well of you, for so their fathers did to the false prophets" (Luke 6:26). Succumbing to the disease of acquiescence exposes us to the charge of being false prophets. The freedom of the pulpit can never be suppressed from without until its possessors destroy it from within.

Chapter II

The Limits and Limitations of Freedom

TRUE FREEDOM IS NEVER ANARCHY, AND THE preacher needs to recognize that there are certain *limits* which may legitimately govern his pronouncements. Many of these are simply the conditions of the environment in which he works. The preacher, therefore, has no right to violate recklessly the limits validly imposed by a situation which also grants him privileges. There are limits outside himself.

Likewise the preacher needs to recognize the *limitations* within himself. If he is genuine and realistic he will have to reckon with them as well.

I

What are the *limits* in the preacher's range of freedom? There are at least four. First there are *ecclesiastical limits*. Most preachers can hardly exist as free-lancers. If a man wants a regular pulpit he will have to work within the structure of a particular ecclesiastical organization. He can never be absolutely free from that frame of reference. He has no right to be commissioned by it and assume its privileges if he is not fundamentally in sympathy with it. A man, for example, has no right to occupy a Methodist pulpit if he does not believe in the episcopal and appointive system. He might criticize the ways in which that system is abused, and he might work with others in an attempt through legal means to modify or amend it, but he has no right to betray it while it exists. On the other hand a Baptist has no right to accept a pulpit in that kind of communion and then denounce the autonomy of the local congregation. Accepting this kind of limit is simply a matter of good sense.

Secondly, there are *doctrinal limits.* Most denominations have doctrinal views to which the preacher is asked to subscribe. It is unthinkable that he could be responsible to that denomination and enjoy its benefits if he were radically and absolutely opposed to them. Certainly there is a legitimate latitude for individual interpretation of time-honored doctrines, but no preacher is free to denounce the entire creed. In the Episcopal Church, for example, he has no right to preach against child baptism. From the strict logic of a denominational system, heresy trials are still proper. Repugnant as they may be to many, a denomination does have the right to set certain doctrinal limits upon the man who accepts its ordination.

Doctrinal limits may seem to precipitate for the preacher a crisis of conscience. No one can force himself to trumpet doctrine against the will of his intellect without inflicting injury upon his integrity. Indeed this crisis is not unknown to many preachers. Still it must be admitted in all honesty that a man's conscience does not take precedence, in every instance, over the rights of doctrine. A communion whose tradition is expressive of certain doctrines has rights too. In this inevitable collision integrity may be sustained on both sides only by the withdrawal of the minister. It is hardly conceivable that the church, as a historic institution, ought to destroy its doctrine in order to preserve the integrity of the preacher. Actually the latter may honor both by humbly resigning.

Thirdly, there are *local limits*. These are the limits of local customs, educational attainments, biblical perspective, and even politics. Differing from place to place, and certainly less sanctified, they are realities which brake a preacher's freedom in the pulpit. In a community of comparatively backward educational attainment, a preacher is hardly at liberty to prepare a sermon as though it were a Ph.D. thesis. Undoubtedly it is the challenge of the preacher to raise the intellectual sights of his people, but it is scarcely appropriate for him to cram the fruits of his seven years of higher education into a single semester of preaching in a local church. Indeed to disregard the local limits of the community in which he operates is to show contempt for the people whom he has been called to serve. Bishop Francis J. McConnell, certainly one of America's greatest prophets, in his Yale lectures on preaching, made this sage observation:

A considerable element of prophetic criticism fails to remind itself that in a church we have to do virtually with a cross-section of a community of a given time. We meet the same varieties of human beings in ecclesiastical as in all other social relationships. Many a prophet seems somehow to feel that a church is an organization standing apart from the usual channels of human experience.[1]

But every church is colored by local interests and relation-

[1] *The Prophetic Ministry* (New York: The Abingdon Press, 1930), p. 260.

ships which interlock it with the characteristics of the community, and no preacher can be very effective if he does not take them into account.

Once while riding on a bus in London I noticed a sign in the driver's compartment, hung directly above his eyes. It read: "This is a double-deck bus." Puzzled, I asked the conductor about it. He stated that some of the London buses were single-deckers and that the drivers—who drove both kinds—had to be reminded lest they drive a double-decker under a too-low bridge. The situation of the preacher is something like this. In the pulpit he is frequently steering a congregation which, because of ecclesiastical, doctrinal, or local limits, cannot be taken down every road that he may want to follow. Perhaps he must find a longer way around to save a crash.

Fourthly, a respectable preacher will observe as limits the canons of *good taste, judgment,* and *discrimination.* The pulpit is no place for loose and lascivious talk. Humor can be nobly and effectively employed, but it can also be puerile and degrading. William Cowper penned a poetic reminder which preachers ought to take seriously:

> He that negotiates between God and man,
> As God's ambassador, the grand concerns
> Of judgment and of mercy, should beware
> Of lightness in his speech. 'Tis pitiful
> To court a grin, when you should woo a soul;
> To break a jest, when pity would inspire
> Pathetic exhortation; and to address
> The skittish fancy with facetious tales,
> When sent with God's commission to the heart.[2]

[2] "The Task," Book II.

The Letter to the Ephesians also sets a high tone for Christian speech: "Let there be no filthiness, nor silly talk, nor levity, which are not fitting; but instead let there be thanksgiving. . . . Let no one deceive you with empty words, for it is because of these things that the wrath of God comes down upon the sons of disobedience" (5:4-6).

The preacher, possessing great freedom in the pulpit, needs in the selection of his words a deft and delicate touch. Restraint, one of the marks of great literature, is an imperative for the preacher. The disciplined use of freedom makes for greater effectiveness, for, as the Greek classicist, Edith Hamilton, has pointed out: "Only the man who holds himself within self-chosen limits can be free."

This means, of course, that the preacher cannot weight his words with ridicule, personal bitterness, or sheer pettiness. These are unquestionably attitudes of small-mindedness which betray not only bad taste but a poverty of soul. Sometimes statements from the pulpit may sound, speciously, like daring and courageous pronouncements, when actually they are not much more than hollow noises indicating the desire of an insecure person to "get back at" someone else. They derive, not from deep conviction, but from bad temper.

Moreover the pulpit is no place for banal comments on the passing scene. It is simply bad taste to deal with petty politics. Once I was embarrassed by a guest in my pulpit who went to great lengths to assure my congregation that the salvation of America lay in the hands of the Republican Party, and that Robert A. Taft would be the next President of the United States. Even the most ardent Republicans present winced at that and one party regular confided to me that he thought the man had spoken in extremely bad taste. Thoreau once gave some advice which serves well for the pulpit: "Read not the Times. Read the Eternities."

Neither is the pulpit well served if it gushes with gossip. If a preacher can be trusted he will not reveal a confidence, no matter how juicily it might spice a sermon. There is sound counsel in Thoreau's famous essay, "Life Without Principle":

If I am to be a thoroughfare, I prefer that it be of the mountain-brooks, the Parnassian streams, and not the town-sewers' . . . I believe the mind can be permanently profaned by the habit of attending to trivial things, so well that all our thoughts shall be tinged with triviality. Our very intellect shall be macadamized, as it were,—its foundation broken into fragments for the wheels of travel to roll over.

Indeed the preacher in the pulpit should serve as a thoroughfare, bearing the traffic of thoughts, tinged, not with triviality, but with the divine. To accomplish this he will need good taste, judgment, and discrimination. He will need to fit the measurements cited by an ancient Greek writer:

> Happy is the man possessing
> The superior holy blessing
> Of a judgment and a taste
> Accurate, refined and chaste.[3]

II

Not only is a preacher restricted by ecclesiastical, doctrinal and local limits, and the canons of good taste—all

[3] Aristophanes, *The Frogs.*

27

imposed upon him from without—but he must face the facts of his own *personal limitations* which are asserted from within.

The preacher is frankly tempted to enjoy a distorted image of himself. Often the object of undue adulation and extravagant expectations concerning his moral, mental, and spiritual powers, he may tend to claim, unconsciously, the virtues assigned to him by admiring parishioners. Still a realistic awareness of himself will keep him constantly mindful that he too suffers from doubts, fears, educational and intellectual inadequacies, and sin. He has no valid freedom to deny, or seem to deny, that he differs in nature from the people to whom he preaches. He must not pretend that his office frees him from normal human limitations.

Here is a thesis about which I have a deep conviction: the preacher actually gains in his freedom to preach to people—to command their respect and attention—when he confesses that he shares with them these limitations. Preaching is deepened, I believe, by this implicit confession. Here a man's basic sincerity is at stake. Authenticity and genuineness mark the utterances of him who evidences the inner struggle. This is what Lowell saw in the great Theodore Parker, for he wrote of him:

> Every word that he speaks has been fierily furnaced
> In the blast of a life that has struggled in earnest.[4]

The great model for the preacher here is Jesus of Nazareth. The experiences of temptation in the wilderness

[4] *Fable for Critics.*

must surely have got into the gospel records because Jesus himself confessed them in his teaching and preaching. Likewise the New Testament as a whole is believable because it is so largely the result of the preaching of the disciples who confessed their cowardice in running away from Jesus when he was taken into custody. The modern preacher of the Christian faith is transmitting a gospel which was first proclaimed with a transparent and rigid honesty. How can he do otherwise?

The late David Roberts once related that he had heard a thoughtful man say that "he did not like going to Church because Christians always take Jesus for granted." Then he added: "I wish sometimes the minister would say something that recalled the days of his own doubts, if he ever had any doubts." Here was a man who could have been communicated with had he heard a preacher possessing the courage to identify himself with the doubts and fears which plague all men. Does a preacher compromise the gospel and dull its thrust when he confesses to doubts and fears? Certainly his preaching will be ineffectual if he has nothing to affirm, but his affirmations will be winged with power if he shows that "every word that he speaks has been fierily furnaced." The power to convince may be related to the willingness to confess. People in the pews are not impressed for long with a preacher who overloads his pronouncements with pretentious claims. Rather real freedom obtains for him who has the humility to say with Paul: "Our knowledge is imperfect and our prophecy is imperfect. . . .Now I know in part" (I Cor. 13:9, 12).

Especially in addressing himself to the painful and perplexing moral issues of the day does the preacher gain access to the attention of his audience when he confesses his participation in unchristian activity. I saw this powerfully demonstrated in a most moving keynote sermon delivered by Bishop Richard C. Raines at the historic Methodist Conference on Human Relations in the early fall of 1959. Facing the painful problems of racial prejudice, Bishop Raines declared that we must, as Christians, take a good square look at ourselves. "We can recognize," he said, "that race prejudice is in all of us. All of us who are members of the white race and all of us who are members of other races." Then he offered this personal confession: "I thought I was free from race prejudice, but a missionary journey to Africa proved to my shame that I was not. The irresistible warmhearted friendliness of the wonderful African people plus the grace of God set me free. But again when our children were about to buy a home I found I was guilty of race prejudice and had to go to my knees." And at that moment I felt that Bishop Raines was *free* to preach to every member of the audience—white man, Negro, Southerner, Northerner. He was free because of frankness.

Undoubtedly this freedom is denied to many preachers because they tend to feel more secure filling the role of the proud and presuming dogmatist. But such posing actually masks the deep-seated insecurity of a man who hasn't the inner courage to confess his lack of omniscience. Ministers might very well take a cue from a great maestro of the musical world, Leonard Bernstein. An observer, writing of him, notes that he never loses his temper at rehearsal. He has even astounded some members of the New York Philharmonic by his willingness to take advice. "Last year, in the David Diamond Symphony," one player reports, "Lenny walked over to the trombone players at the end of a rehearsal. 'Did I give you a wrong cue?' he asked, kind of worried. The idea is, Lenny was not afraid to admit that he might have goofed. Brother, that ain't insecurity. That's *security*." [5] Similarly, a preacher's freedom in the pulpit is based on that kind of security. The preacher is obviously insecure when he finds it hard to admit that he is an ordinary human being. But the preacher who finds a place in his preaching for the honest confession of his own limitations has free access to the intellectual highways of his listeners.

[5] "What Bernstein Is Doing to the Philharmonic," *Harper's Magazine*, May 9, 1959, p. 47.

Chapter III

The Necessity of Intellectual Toil

No one in our society possesses greater freedom to speak his mind than the preacher. Yet this freedom is frequently abused because he has so little to say. His claim to freedom is baseless when pap is all he can produce in the pulpit. Like a noisy gong or a clanging cymbal he may proclaim his freedom, but mere loudness cannot fill his words with meaning.

It is plain that there is a corollary to the preacher's freedom: the necessity of intellectual toil. No one can harvest a crop of homiletical fruits on Sunday who has not spent the week in plowing, seeding, and cultivating his mind. He who preaches off the top of his head is misusing his freedom. The preacher has no rights in the pulpit which can be won without hard intellectual labor. This necessity requires serious reflection. Several considerations are in order.

I

To begin with, the freedom to preach effectively in any pulpit necessitates a prior freedom: the freedom to study. Any church desiring good preaching from its minister ought to understand the ground rules. No man can consistently deliver good sermons if the congregation does not perceive the necessity for his having the time to study. It does not do much good to grant the preacher freedom in the pulpit if he is not also given freedom of *time* to prepare. Preaching takes time; preparation for preaching takes *much more* time. A congregation mocks the freedom of the pulpit if it keeps its minister so busy that he has no time to study. In interviewing a prospective candidate for its pulpit, a pulpit committee might very well ask, "How much time do you spend in study and sermon preparation?" Then it should be announced that the committee will use its authority to guard and defend the preacher's study from unwarranted intrusions. This prior freedom must be guaranteed by the congregation.

Most of our churches, of course, are not conditioned at the present time to initiate this freedom. Hence the preacher may have to demand it as a practical necessity and a sacred right. It is the best way he has of honoring both pulpit and people.

II

I also suggest that both the congregation and the preacher ought to regard his role as that of a *thinker*. In earlier times the clergyman occupied a place of intellectual prominence in the community. He was one of its most learned men, one of its most respected thinkers. Our more recent history has transmuted his role into that of "pastoral-director" of an increasingly complex organization. No longer is he regarded as the purveyor of cultural and intellectual values. This is lamentable because no one else in our society is called upon by the nature of his profession to deal more in the realm of ideas. The preacher in the pulpit is seeking to explore the inscrutable, to penetrate the mysterious, to describe the ineffable. To fulfill this assignment requires immense intellectual effort. He must have skill in the handling of ideas. As the translator and transformer of infinite thought he must be respected as a thinker.

Unfortunately too many preachers are like the senator referred to by Halford Luccock. When asked what he thought of a certain issue, he said: "I haven't time to think. I have to make a speech." If a man is going to preach he *has* to think. And if he hasn't got the time or disposition to think he hasn't got the right to preach. Simone Weil in her book *The Need for Roots* spoke a revelant word: "There has been a lot of freedom of thought over the past few years," she declared, "but no thought. Rather like the case of a child who not having any meat, asks for salt with which to season it."

Though not a theologian in the technical sense, a preacher must certainly think theologically. His privilege is that of proclaiming the nature and the ways of God to men. To do this he must think the great thoughts about God. He needs to share the insight of T. S. Eliot who once described theology as "a masculine discipline." The mind grappling with the issues of theology must be masculine and hard working. Words, empty words, come easily and without ceasing, but words bearing the freight of meaning, ring authentically with the notes of thought. Frances Minturn Howard has perceived this truth brilliantly:

> Beneath the flow of words
> Light as lifted hair

Colored by the sun,
Articulate with air,

There moves the bone of thought,
Socketed and clear,
On its fine-tooled joint
White, remote, austere.

Delight who will the smooth
Artifice of tongue,
The silver-bodied core
On which the flesh is hung

Is sweeter to the eye
That sees the naked skull
Luminous beneath
And knows it beautiful.[1]

The late Archbishop William Temple, in his great theological work, *Nature, Man and God,* related this "bone of thought" to theology in another figure by conceiving of the relationship between mind and reality as being like that between a key and lock. The mind, he said, is like a key that unlocks the meaning of reality. And, like the key fitting the lock, it fits reality, because both were made by the same Locksmith. If the mind of the preacher is like this key, it must be sharply tooled, sturdy and ever active. One of America's greatest preachers and thinkers was George A. Gordon of Boston. A pronouncement was made in his autobiography which is just and fitting: "Let there

[1] Copyright, 1944 by Contemporary Poetry. From the book *All Keys Are Glass* by Frances Minturn Howard. Published 1950 by E. P. Dutton & Co., Inc. and reprinted with their permission.

35

be everlasting scorn for those who say because a man is a minister he cannot be a thinker; let there be the same scorn for those who meekly accept this indignity." [2]

III

It is essential for the preacher to realize that there is freedom in knowledge. A man is not free to practice law if he does not *know* the law. A man is not free to practice medicine and surgery if he does not *know* biology, physiology, anatomy, and so forth. Just so the preacher is not free to preach the gospel unless he *knows* the gospel.

At the age of eighteen I made my decision to enter the ministry. This decision was generated in a powerfully emotional experience at a summer youth institute. As I returned to my home that summer the engines of emotion churned with the desire to preach. I was so eager to preach that I would have seized any opportunity at any time and at any place. Very soon opportunities were offered to me but I made a discomforting discovery: I was really not *free* to preach because I knew so little about the Christian faith. I was in fact enslaved by a vast ignorance of the gospel. My speech might blaze with emotion but when the smoke had cleared there was no recognizable trace of real knowledge. For a while I suffered from what the great Justice Learned Hand called "False assurance, that grows from pride in our powers and ignorance of our ignorance." This ignorance was dispelled when I discovered that I had no freedom to convince, not even myself. Then I knew that there lay ahead of me a lifetime process of learning what the gospel was all about. Since that time I have felt really

[2] *My Education and Religion*, pp. 322-23.

free only when I have taken the trouble to *know* what I am talking about. One thing is certain: I will never be completely free because I will never know enough about the Bible, theology, and the history of the church.

Shoddy preparation, therefore, may fatally limit a preacher's freedom to convince his congregation. One of the greatest laymen I know, bountifully instructed in the knowledge of the Christian faith, brilliant in his own profession, confided to me once that he exacted one requirement from every preacher he listened to: he must know the facts about the subject on which he is speaking. A preacher simply is not free to preach to such a thoughtful layman if he distorts the facts. On the other hand the preacher who has equipped himself with knowledge-in-depth of his subject is free to command this man's attention. Knowledge *is* power, and freedom!

IV

Intellectual toil is required for the achievement of *clarity* in the preacher's presentation of his message. Obviously no man is free to communicate with people if he is not capable of making himself clear. This is not a gift to be taken for granted. Most preachers do not have it to begin with. The achievement of it is an art, much like that of a great musician who spends endless hours in practice.

The preacher with the capacity to speak simply and clearly to ordinary people is like a transformer that takes the powerful current from a high voltage line and steps it down for the domestic user. Just as high-voltage current must be stepped down for ordinary use, so the great truths of religion must be made simple and useful for ordinary people. The great masters of the pulpit—men like Phillips Brooks, George A. Gordon, Henry Ward Beecher, Harry Emerson Fosdick, and Ralph W. Sockman—have achieved this clarity. Hence they have been magnificently free to preach to ordinary men and women. Yet no one of them has attained this freedom without unremitting toil in his study. The study room of this kind of preacher is like a powerful transformer, heated by the excitement and intensity of intellectual and spiritual activity.

Lyman Beecher once said that "eloquence is logic on fire." Natural eloquence is given to very few. Most preachers must strive for it; he who acquires it has surely subjected himself to mental discipline. For this reason I have always believed that the study of philosophy and its sister discipline, logic, are protein requirements in the preacher's intellectual diet. The mastery of these, plus the fervency of soul-deep convictions, incandesces his interpretation of the gospel.

Without this intellectual toil the preacher tends to obscure rather than open the scriptures. Then the precious time allotted the preacher is ill-used. E. B. White, writing about *The Elements of Style,* asserts that "muddiness is not merely a disturber of prose, it is a destroyer of life, of hope." He who preaches so that his message is muddied has renounced the freedom of the pulpit. The cost of clarity is a commitment to intellectual toil.

V

It ought to be pointed out that there is a great difference between "sounding off" in the pulpit and *persuading* men and women to change their lives. The preacher may use his freedom to "sound off" but the freedom to persuade is quite another matter. It takes an inquiring, muscular mind to quicken and energize the minds of others. As a thoughtful layman once said to me, "The freedom of the pulpit must not be construed to mean the freedom to bore."

The preacher ought never forget that his freedom is emphatically conditioned by the listener's prerogative to tune out his channel. The late Bernard DeVoto, in analyzing the effectiveness of the novel, offered an observation which is equally applicable to the sermon:

If you are caught at a dinner where some bore drones on, uttering dreary commonplaces, proving himself insensitive to human experience and too stupid to respond to it, you have no recourse. But if you pick up a novel and find that its author is such a person, you can stop reading. Why shouldn't you? You are interested in people, not in cardboard characters that have been pulped in skimmed milk. You are interested in emotion but not aridity or sentimentality, in thinking but not in obvious or false or dull thinking. You are grateful for any insight into the nature or meaning of experience that anyone can give you but the intelligence at work here is fumbling and blind, the imagination poverty-stricken. Certainly you can stop reading.[3]

The man in the pew may be trapped by trifles once, or even several times, but it is likely that he will eventually exert his right to be absent or, if present through loyal duty, to take a mental nap. In either case the preacher has no freedom to persuade.

There is an old saying that "the empty vessel makes

[3] "Why Read Dull Novels?" *Harper's Magazine,* Feb., 1952, pp. 66-69.

the greatest sound." Alexander Pope, recognizing this, once
said that "it is with narrow-souled people as with narrow-
necked bottles; the less they have in them the more noise
they make in pouring out." Add to this an observation of
a Frenchman, La Bruyére, that "one of the signs of
mediocrity of mind is the habit of always telling stories."
All of these are examples of the preacher merely "sounding off" in the pulpit, abusing his freedom because he has
not toiled in the vineyards of the mind. In Ecclesiastes there
is a proverb which could be used as a commentary on much
preaching:

> If the iron is blunt, and one does not
>   whet the edge,
> he must put forth more strength;
> but wisdom helps one to succeed.
>
> (10:10)

Certainly if a sermon is dull, and the preacher obviously
has not sharpened its thrust through the discipline of his
mind, he must jab the harder in striving for a point. If
only he understood that to *persuade* he must commit himself to the stewardship of intelligence.

VI

Finally, the preacher must be warned that the cost of
enduring freedom of the pulpit is a life-long devotion to
study. The figure of the preacher suffering in his middle
years from intellectual palsy is familiar and pathetic. Freedom of the pulpit is banished for the man who loses his
excitement for the world of ideas.

The Necessity of Intellectual Toil

The terrible temptation and tendency for most preachers, with the passing of the years, is to become so busily engaged in the organizational activities of the church, and to become so hopelessly enmeshed in its operational machinery, that they allow their intellectual life to be strangled. More and more he finds himself functioning as a minder of the machinery while relinquishing his calling as the minister of men's minds. The prevention of this slow deadening of the mental arteries will require a massive force of will and a monumental commitment. With every passing day of his ministry—especially if he is effective and influential—he will have to fight with all his might to maintain the strict discipline of his study. He will have to believe the truth of Christopher Morley's notation that "Nothing ages people like not thinking."

It is my conviction that in an enduring pastorate a congregation will listen to the preacher whose sermons evidence intellectual toil, research, and thoughtfulness.

Chapter IV

The Catalyst of Courage

THE PULPIT IS NOT LIKE THE FLOOR OF THE United States Congress. A congressman may take that floor and say anything he pleases. The laws of the land protect him from suits of libel or slander. The preacher has no such immunity. Especially as a Protestant he realizes that he will be held responsible for everything he says. Hence the fervor of his convictions may sometimes get cooled in the cold knowledge that counterattack is possible. In such a moment, when courage fails, the preacher is not free.

Sometimes we say of a certain kind of person, "He has the courage of his convictions." This saying seems to imply that a person can have convictions *without* courage. Indeed, convictions may be so confined to the inward sphere that they seldom register in the outward witness. Many persons have strong inner attitudes which they are afraid to express. Preachers frequently lack the courage to proclaim their convictions from the pulpit. Without this courage a preacher cannot grasp the freedom of the pulpit and make the gospel of Christ a live issue of the day. Where there is no courage available, convictions limp. Hence, many pulpits are lamed because convictions have no more force than mere opinions.

The Catalyst of Courage

But when courage is present in the pulpit it serves as a catalyst. Just as certain chemical reactions are very markedly accelerated in the presence of substances known as "catalysts," so the performance of the preacher is energized and nerved by the presence of courage. What would otherwise be hapless and hopeless convictions are transmitted into throbbing power. The preacher who fits John Hutton's definition of the prophet as "A man who, in the name of God, boldly contradicts the spirit of his time," will have to call upon an enabling power. He may *want* to do so, and the emotion for doing so may surge within. But, until there is something like this chemical reaction, his heart will quake and his voice will quiver. Merely to possess the freedom to speak is not enough. Elmer W. Shaw makes this clear in lines to which he gives the title "Free Will":

> For burrowing moles and termites
> Reactions are quite certain—
> Blind automatons and slaves
> Behind an iron curtain.
> But I, with the gift of freedom,
> Can make my own provision,
> Eased of instinct and restraint
> But plagued by indecision! [1]

In a theoretical sense every preacher is free, but freedom leads nowhere until the sluggish stream of indecision is accelerated by the catalyst of courage.

Courage, for the preacher, is a catalytic agent in the attainment of freedom which distinguishes his preaching on three accounts.

[1] The *New York Times*, April 24, 1955.

I

Courage enables the preacher to be his own true self while following the dictates of his own heart. It takes courage for a man to be himself and a "man of courage" acts with *heart*. Indeed, courage grows out of the heart of a man. The pusillanimous person, on the other hand, is one who is weak and timid because he is "small in mind." But the man of courage is large in both heart and mind. These are the inner qualities which, like catalytic agents, transform convictions from cringing withdrawals into manly witness. Such a man possesses the heart and mind to screw his courage to the sticking point. Without them the freedom of the pulpit sags.

The ancient Hebrews looked upon the heart as the source of understanding, love, pleasure, and courage. "Keep your heart with all vigilance," said one of the writers of Proverbs, "For from it flow the springs of life" (4:23). In one sense this is the sum and substance of all preaching. It indicates as well the location of a preacher's own courage. Paul Tillich certainly referred to the preacher's deepest need in his book, *The Courage to Be*. The preacher, if he is to exercise freedom, must above all else have the courage to be himself. In these days when conformity creeps paralyzingly into the very heart of individuality a man must fight for the preservation of his own integrity. Words spoken from the pulpit are but hollow echoes of mere conventionality if they do not bear the unmistakable ring of personal authenticity. And to be one's own true self in the pulpit takes courage. The lack of courage results in captivity.

How does one manifest this "courage to be" himself? Several years ago the celebrated playwright, Arthur Miller, wrote an article in which he declared a principle for serious writers which applies with equal relevance to the preacher. In explaining his own adaptation of Ibsen's play, *An Enemy of the People,* he wrote:

> There is one quality in Ibsen that no serious writer can afford to overlook. It lies in the very center of his force, and I found in it—as I hope others will—a profound source of strength. It is his insistence, his utter conviction, that he is going to say what he has to say, and that the audience is going to listen. It is the very same quality that makes a star actor, a great public speaker, and a lunatic. Every Ibsen play begins with the unwritten words: "Now listen here!" [2]

Certainly the preacher who occupies a free pulpit, and who is himself occupied by the courage to be himself, begins every sermon with the assumption of the right to says: "Now listen here!" Perhaps George Bernard Shaw made his heroine in "Saint Joan" speak as distinctively for the preacher as for herself when she replies to the Dauphin just after he has said that he has no wish but to be left alone: "I have a message to thee from God; and thou must listen to it, though thy heart break with the terror of it." The preacher, striving for personal integrity, will have to call upon the catalyst of courage for two reasons: First, because he will, in all probability, be speaking to the sub-

[2] *New York Times* Drama Section, Dec. 24, 1950.

terranean hostility of a crowd which does not wish to be spoken to in that manner; and second, because to claim to have a message from God is so daringly presumptuous and preposterous as to cause a rational, mortal man to quail. Still it *is* the function of the preacher to speak for God. Only the man who feels the terror of that responsibility will recognize his need for courage.

If a preacher is to proclaim truly the gospel of Jesus Christ these days he is going to feel, on certain occasions, that he is terribly alone. Possibly he will need the courage of the early Methodist circuit riders who followed the raw and ever-moving frontier across the vast, unexplored American continent. These were simple, often unlettered men, raw-boned, and virile, whose flaming tongues were matched by steel nerves and hearts of undauntable faith. On many occasions their true nature was boldly revealed as they faced the angry violence of drunken and irresponsible mobs. The exploits of our synthetic television cowboys pale in comparison. Their inspiration for valor came, of course, from their intrepid leader, John Wesley. His frontier preachers endured the hardships and hostilities of the wilderness because they took seriously his advice: "Always look a mob in the face." Wesley did not give this advice from the plush safety of a parlor. Rather he reflected the courage of his own heart which never blanched in the many personal encounters he had with fierce and brutal mobs. Halford Luccock has found references in Wesley's Journal to sixty riots which were stirred up by his preaching. He also cites the testimony of journalist William T. Stead, who observed that Wesley would have made a much smaller impression on history "without that marvellous body, with muscles of whipcord, with lungs of leather, and the heart of a lion." Without that kind of heart a man cannot stand alone to be himself.

The modern preacher may not think of himself as addressing a mob. Still, a congregation can be well-dressed, well-fed, well-housed, well-mannered and still be seething with hostility. It takes immense courage these days, for example, for a preacher to look his congregation in the face and declare that racial segregation is a sin. From such pronouncements many congregations are currently recoiling in wrath. Yet, here and there, there are preachers who refuse to be throttled down to the idling purr of innocuous and insipid sayings in the midst of raging evils. Undoubtedly, preachers of this caliber have read, and taken seriously, the words of God heard by Ezekiel:

"But the house of Israel will not listen to you; for they are not willing to listen to me; because all the house of Israel are of a hard forehead and a stubborn heart. Behold, I have made your face hard against their faces, and your forehead hard against their forehead . . . *fear them not, nor be dismayed at their looks,* for they are a rebellious house." Moreover he said to me, "Son of man, all my words that I shall speak to you receive in your heart and hear with your ears. And go, get you to the exiles, to your people, and say to them, 'Thus says the Lord God'; whether they hear or refuse to hear." (3:7-11)

To look a mob in the face, and not "be dismayed at their looks," requires "the heart of a lion."

Therein lies the real nature of the prophet. Every prophet from Amos to Jesus has had to stand alone, defying the gibbet and the mob. Neither do modern-day prophets escape this stern requirement. Comparatively few can endure this aloneness. Where it exists, pusillanimity in the pulpit is evidence of the heart and mind which are too small to bear up alone under opposition. Hence, there is no assumption of freedom. The freedom of the pulpit requires the capacity defined by Paul Tillich: "The courage to be as oneself is the courage to follow reason and to defy irrational authority."

II

Let us consider what it is that actually arouses the wrath of a congregation against a preacher. Obviously a congregation will not react in a hostile manner against the preacher who deals in broad and glittering generalities. Platitudes do not often provoke a group of people to wrath. Clichés may move an audience to boredom but not to an embittered clash with the speaker. Sadly enough it is only when a preacher becomes relevant and specific that people resent him. It has been observed that modern congregations love to hear sermons condemning the sins of Abraham, Isaac, and Jacob, but that they twist uncomfortably when the word sin is so pointedly interpreted as to cover the "organizational man" and the "man in the gray flannel suit." They prefer a discussion of sin in the abstract and not in the concrete. James Russell Lowell provides us with a diagnosis:

> I'm willin' a man should go tollable strong
> Agin wrong in the abstract, fer that kind o' wrong
> Is ollers unpop'lar an' never gits pitied,
> Because it's a crime no one ever committed;

48

But he mus'n't be hard on partickler sins,
Coz then he'll be kickin' the people's own shins.[3]

Perhaps one of the most sincere and serious attacks on the preacher's freedom has come from Clarence B. Randall, a highly respected churchman and chairman of the board of Inland Steel. Mr. Randall, who has been himself sharply criticized by fellow businessmen who regard him as too liberal, has nonetheless demanded that preachers desist from "social action" pronouncements. In his book, *Freedom's Faith*, Mr. Randall declares that the church is "holy because it stands serenely above all controversy." He also reveals that "the businessman wants no politics from his minister. Not for a moment does he wish to restrict his pastor from exercising his own privileges as a citizen by entering freely into every phase of American debate, but he expects him to come down out of the pulpit to do it." [4] Surely Mr. Randall is right in expecting his minister to take off his clerical gown when engaging in precinct politics, but would he tie the preacher's tongue in the pulpit when it comes to facing the overwhelming moral problems of our society? Can he really believe that the church is "holy because it stands serenely above all controversy"? Has he never heard of Amos, Hosea, Isaiah, Jeremiah, and Jesus who spoke of specific sins? Are preachers to keep silent while the specific, though controversial, evils of racism, nuclear poisoning, and alcoholism rage in the world? Just because every moral evil in the world gets entangled in politics is the preacher required to wash his

[3] *Biglow Papers*, 1st Series, No IV.
[4] (Boston: Little, Brown and Co.), p. 173.

hands of all moral concern, and while wrapped warmly in his holy robes strikes a pose of utter serenity and generality far above the battle? If this is what men like Mr. Randall really expect and obtain from their preachers, then the pulpit is not free.

Upon considering the demand for silence made by a sophisticated and well-meaning Christian of the high caliber of Mr. Randall, the preacher shudders and wonders if he can possibly command the courage to preach the gospel relevantly and specifically. If he has read the Holy Bible and regards its contents as a handbook for modern preaching, he wonders how he can "stand serenely above all controversy" and at the same time be true to the great prophets who related their messages to the specific sins of robbing the poor, oppressing widows and orphans, graft and corruption in business, and nefarious foreign alliances. How can he be true to the apostle Paul who by his preaching threatened the lucrative business of idol manufacture, who raised a storm of controversy over false teachers and preachers? And how can he be true to Jesus who shattered the peace of his home-town synagogue at Nazareth, who condemned the unctuous piety of the religious and the greedy desires of the privileged, who drove the money-changers from the temple? What is there left for the modern preacher to preach if he has to be so serene as to be senselessly unaware of what is happening in the world? To accept this role a preacher would have to turn tail and run from every specific issue. He would be a coward, glowing with geniality, but afraid of the precise pronouncement which says, "Thou ailest *here!*"

The preachers who have made history have never been

serene! Neither have they been innocuously imprecise!
Allan Knight Chalmers, professor of preaching and applied
Christianity at Boston University School of Theology,
frequently refers to what he calls "the charter" of the
Broadway Tabernacle of New York City, a church he once
served with distinction. It was first stated by the first great
preacher of that church, Joseph P. Thompson. One day
Thompson had been shot at from the balcony by a fanatic
who was enraged by his preaching on a great social-moral
evil of that day. Thompson, called "The Little Giant of
Broadway" by a newspaper reporter, did not even duck.
But standing straight in the pulpit he opened his mouth
to say: "The man who stands in this pulpit must be the
first to see, the first to feel, the first to move against all
forms of moral evil in the world." That utterance would
seem to be faithful to the same charge which Ezekiel heard
coming to him from the mouth of God:

But if the watchman sees the sword coming and does not
blow the trumpet, so that people are not warned, and the
sword comes, and takes any one of them; that man is taken
away in his iniquity, but his blood I will require at the watchman's hands. So you, son of man, I have made a watchman for
the house of Israel; whenever you hear a word from my mouth,
you shall give them warning from me. (33:6, 7.)

Shall the preacher who has been called to speak for God
in the twentieth century be guilty of the sin of the silent
trumpet?

Behind the Iron Curtain in East Germany the clergy
are kept under an unceasing and ever-mounting attack.
Yet, not long ago *The Christian Century* reported that

the pastors were being ordered to stay with their congregations. Bishop Gottfried Noth of Dresden advised his pastors not to let their message be confined to "the sphere of piety" alone. "It's the duty of a pastor," he wrote, "to tell the congregation what God wants that congregation to do, in the circumstances in which it finds itself today." For many pastors that is a daring and possibly fatal assumption of freedom. How could it be accomplished without courage? Courage in that sense would have to be a catalyst of massive size and power.

Throughout this exploration of the nature of courage I have been employing a term borrowed from chemistry. Besides being an agent which controls a chemical reaction, either by acceleration or deceleration, a catalyst has another characteristic which enriches the idea of courage. The catalyst agent is not *consumed* in the process, but is available for further use upon demand. This suggests the tough and durable quality which belongs to courage. Once a man commands the courage of his convictions in any given situation he usually finds that he has become empowered by an inner resource which is available for further witness. Courage, once employed, begets courage. It is not exhausted in a single stand. It becomes an essential catalyst in the pulpit because the preacher of prophetic insight must have an unquenchable supply of courage if he is to explore with his congregation the specific implications of the gospel.

III

In the third place, it is the catalyst of courage which enables the preacher to give "the last full measure of devotion" to Christ. Though the Protestant Christian pulpit is in principle free, every preacher who is worth his salt and truly committed to Christ must be prepared in ultimate circumstances to pay a price for this freedom. Though the preacher is free to preach as God gives him light, he must not expect to be free of all consequences of that preaching. Many of the great prophets of history, with Jesus standing above all, have had to pay a stiff price.

Once when I was preparing a youth class for church membership, a boy, in reciting the books of the New Testament, said "Collisions" instead of "Colossians." I have often thought that he quite inadvertently supplied an insight into the nature of the New Testament. By the faithful proclamation of the gospel, and especially by its specific applications to our time, a man is going to collide with opposition. The man who takes a crucial stand must expect to get hurt. Though the prophet of God is certainly a critic of his times, it does not necessarily follow, as I heard a wise layman once observe, that every critic is a prophet. Some want to criticize without cost. But the critic who is also a prophet expects to pay a price. The true preacher is realistic enough to know that he may come to the place where he must say with Martin Luther: "My conscience is captive to the Word of God. I cannot and I will not recant anything, for to go against conscience is neither right nor safe. Here I stand, I cannot do otherwise, God help me. Amen."

One preacher I know dared to "stare a mob in the face" and say that segregation is a sin. The mob rushed at him hatefully. They surrounded his car, spitting epithets of rage. Threats of death came consistently for days on end.

In the end he won a qualified victory, but the final blow was a boycott of the church budget. He made no defense, asked for none. He simply removed himself quietly, sacrificing his own position rather than allowing the church to be entirely destroyed. His last sermon was on "The Freedom of the Pulpit." In a letter to me relating his experiences he said: " 'Freedom of the Pulpit' might require bags being all ready every Sunday at noon." Can the prophetic preacher ever expect any permanent security in this world? Can he ever completely unpack his bags?

The acceptance of the answer to that question requires courage. That there are costly consequences to preaching was impressed upon me in 1954 when I attended the Evanston Assembly of the World Council of Churches. Among the delegates from all over the world were some of the great modern heroes of the faith. Not a few bore in their lives "the marks of Jesus," having witnessed through tyranny and terror. Not a few had come to Evanston at great personal risk. I shall never forget the way a young preacher, John Havea of the Tonga Islands, caught the high drama of the moment at the early worship service which opened the Assembly. Substituting for Methodist Bishop Lew of Korea who was unable to appear, he began his sermon by saying that he found himself with the rare privilege of Simon of Cyrene, that of bearing the cross for Bishop Lew, as Simon had borne it for Christ. Ever since I have thought of preaching as the privilege of bearing the cross for Christ. And, if the Cross has been a catalyst of human history, affecting every century and every people, how can we, who preach in his name, do without the catalyst of courage?

Chapter V

The Eloquence of Love

MARTIN LUTHER MADE MANY TRENCHANT COM-
mentaries on the preaching art, but I would dare to suggest that in one he was wrong. Once he declared: "When
a man first comes into the pulpit, he is much perplexed to
see so many heads before him. When I stand there I look
upon none, but imagine they are all blocks that are set
before me." [1] It is my belief that this impersonal attitude is
a factor in severely limiting the freedom of the preacher.
Make no mistake about it: the congregation will readily
discern that the preacher is measuring them as though they
were blocks. And they will not be flattered.

On the other hand, Alexander V. G. Allen, the biog-
rapher of Phillips Brooks, properly perceives the freedom
of this magnetic preacher's hold upon his hearers when he
notes:

He loved places and things, he loved nature, but above all
he loved humanity. It was this gift which made his heart leap
up when he beheld the waiting congregation. No one can

[1] *The Table Talk of Martin Luther,* Thomas S. Kepler, ed. (Cleveland:
World Publishing Co.) , p. 224.

forget the look that he gave when he had ascended the pulpit, as if to draw in the inspiration for the effect that was to follow before he bent himself with the fervor and tumult of his powerful soul to the communication of his message.[2]

What a difference there is between looking coldly upon blocks and lovingly upon people! Phillips Brooks was one of the greatest preachers ever to stand in a pulpit. His sermons were impassioned utterances, majestically storming the stoniest hearts, overwhelming with fluency and grace. But his greatest source of eloquence was his love. No preacher ever loved humanity more, and no preacher was ever freer to preach. We will do well to consider carefully the freeing power which derives from the preacher's heartfelt love for his people.

I

For one thing, many preachers are really not free in the pulpit because the gospel of love they preach is to them more an abstraction than a reality to which they can give heartfelt expression. They may be earnest but unloving and unfeeling.

Alfred North Whitehead once described the detachment of the scholar from real life as "the celibacy of the intellect." For the preacher there is often a kind of "celibacy of love." He preaches about love, his words may ornately define and describe love, but he does not really know love. He may recommend love as the salvation of the world, but he is in his own heart tepid when it comes to loving. Phyllis McGinley has aptly limned such a person in these lines which she calls "The Old Reformer":

[2] *The Life of Phillips Brooks,* Vol. II, p. 185.

Few friends he kept that pleased his mind,
His marriage failed when it began,
Who worked unceasing for mankind
But loathed his fellow man.[3]

This same feeling was expressed recently by one of my favorite characters, Linus, in the priceless comic strip, "Peanuts." A little girl scorns Linus who has just announced his chosen profession: "You a doctor! Ha! That's a big laugh! You could never be a doctor! You know why? Because you don't love mankind, that's why!" To which Linus hotly replies: "I love mankind . . . it's *people* I can't stand!" [4] There are not a few men in the ministry who love mankind as an abstraction, but who cannot stand *people*. In preaching this feeling cannot be hidden. It will assert itself as a chain on interpersonal relationships in the parish and as a chill on words in the pulpit.

Phillips Brooks never saw his congregation as a collection of human abstractions. We are well instructed by this invaluable insight which he shared with the preaching fraternity in his famous *Lectures on Preaching:*

There is a power which lies at the centre of all success in preaching, and whose influence reaches out to the circumference, and is essential everywhere. Without its presence we cannot imagine the most brilliant talents making a preacher of the Gospel in the fullest sense. Where it is largely present, it is wonderful how many deficiencies count for nothing. It has the characteristics which belong to all the most essential powers. . . . Without this power, preaching is almost sure to become either a struggle of ambition or a burden of routine. With it, preaching is an ever fresh delight. The power is the value of the human soul, felt by the preacher, and inspiring all his work.[5]

Surely the preacher who feels this value of the human soul each time he preaches achieves an eloquence which can never be realized by him who detaches the gospel of love from living persons. There is freedom in love for persons, only aridity in abstracted love. As Rabbi Stephen S. Wise has said, once again, brilliantly: "The eloquence of the lips may be silver; the eloquence of a life is ever golden. Every other service of the preacher may be doubted, but a life is irresistible in its influence."

II

Possibly the real reason for the inability of many preachers to enrich their messages with the nuances of love is their personal insecurity. One of the most striking preachers I know ultimately leaves me cold and unconvinced because I see behind the brilliant façade of his words the shivering presence of his own insecurity. Greater facility and fluency with words are given to few, but when one knows something about his personal relationships with his peers and parishioners his words impress one as being more ornamental than profound. Needing always to be at the center of the stage, hurting and hindering those who tend to threaten his position, he frequently exposes his own insecurity. So as a preacher he is admired but not loved, for he has no power in his preaching to beget love.

[5] P. 255.

It is interesting at this point to note, perhaps, a significant difference between the "loquacious" person and the "eloquent" person. Both of these words stem from the same root: *loquor*, meaning "speak." The "loquacious" person "talks too much," while an "eloquent" person "speaks out." Might we say that the loquacious preacher, then, talks too much because he feels compelled to cover his haunting insecurity with a waterfall of words, whereas the truly eloquent preacher *speaks out* of a heart of love? The difference is that the man who deeply loves his people is inwardly mature and secure.

Most of the familiar poses of the preacher, then—the "stuffed shirt," the insufferably pious one, the man who cannot relate well to other members of his staff—are varying disguises of the inmost heart which is not really capable of love. Hence the lack of freedom in the pulpit. The only cure for this, of course, is the imaginative heart schooled in the requirements of Christlike love.

III

The most important insight into the eloquence of love remains to be stated. The freedom of the pulpit must be exercised with love because in his prophetic role the preacher is confronting his people with the truth, and, as everyone knows, the truth often hurts. "Rightly handling the word of truth," in Paul's phrase, implies the need for special skills. Freedom, in this sense, is based on the skill of love.

There are many times when a preacher feels himself pitted in his pronouncements against the views of his people. If he does not then speak to them in love, if he has not loved them in all of the dimensions of his ministry, he hasn't a chance of being heard and heeded. Just as no parent can scold or spank a child for very long, and have that child accept the judgment brought against him, if he has not also experienced the abundance of his parent's love, a preacher cannot proclaim the truth that hurts if his people do not know that he speaks in love. But let him go with his people through the valleys of fear and sorrow, let him climb with them to the peaks of life's joys, let him live with them and know them and be their loving minister, and they will listen to him respectfully in whatever he has to say. I once heard the late Joseph M. M. Gray declare it to be his faith that a minister could in time change the climate of a congregation's thinking if he would only preach to them out of a pastorate of love. These lines of Henry Barnett, entitled "I Heard a Prophet," illustrate the truth:

> I bowed to his words: they gathered; they broke
> Over cowering conscience and impulse; they drove
> In echoes of passion that cried in their pain,
> The thunder that follows the lightnings of love.[6]

The thunder of prophetic preaching can resound in the hearts of men only if it is preceded by "the lightnings of love." For "if I have prophetic powers, and understand all mysteries and all knowledge, and if I have all faith, so as to remove mountains, but have not love, I am nothing."

David Wesley Soper has suggested that the necessary command of the gospel, "Repent, and believe," is like "the

---

[6] *motive*, Oct. 1951, p. 31. Used by permission.

sound of a hammer on cold iron." Indeed the human heart in all of its pride and passion tends to resent the bluntness of that command. But as Soper continues: "The iron must be heated to be malleable. To hammer on cold metal is to create nothing but noise. The artist, hammering on white-hot metal, may bend it to his will." [7] Soper avers that "much preaching hammers noisily on cold metal because it evades the question: 'What must I do to be saved?,'" and of course he is right. But the primary deficiency may lie less in the evasion of this question than in the lack of the preacher's love. The preacher who is sufficiently eloquent to unlock the hearts and minds of his people to hear this offensive gospel is adept at turning the key of love.

If he tries to hammer home the gospel without this love, he must bear the sting of resentment. Several years ago I was struck by a sentence a critic had written in his review of a Broadway play. Of the playwright he said: "The fault is that he has been so much concerned with how his play would perform that he has thought little of how it would communicate. His back is to the audience." How often does the preacher preach with his back to the audience? How contemptuous he may be as he handles the painful words of truth! He who preaches with his back to the people fails in communication because he obviously does not love them.

Once again I believe Martin Luther was only half right when he recommended for those who were "hardened, obstinate, stiff-necked, and rebel-hearted": "these hard

[7] *Epistle to the Skeptics* (New York: Association Press), p. 91.

heads need sound knocks." Indeed prophetic preaching does deliver "sound knocks," but not without "the lightnings of love."

To know what is fitting for fulfilling his role as prophet, the preacher needs to preface his pronouncements with the words of Paul: "I am speaking the truth in Christ" (Rom. 9:1). And how can any preacher preach Christ who does not preach in love? The love of Christ is eloquent. It illumines every utterance. Without it no one is free to preach.

Chapter VI

In Whose Service Is Perfect Freedom

WHENEVER I THINK ABOUT THE FREEDOM OF THE preacher there runs through my mind like a constant refrain a familiar phrase. It is from a collect for peace in the Book of Common Prayer: "O God, who art the author of peace and lover of concord, in knowledge of whom standeth our eternal life, *whose service is perfect freedom;* Defend us thy humble servants in all assaults of our enemies; that we, surely trusting in Thy defence, may not fear the power of any adversaries, through the might of Jesus Christ our Lord." This phrase, frequently used in other prayers, locates an important ground of the preacher's freedom to preach.

That freedom would be very fleeting indeed if the preacher did not seek in his own life to reveal God through his service. This is a truth most clearly written in the New Testament. The preacher who would be free in his utterances needs to reflect most seriously upon the nature of his role as servant to his people. On his human side the minister may not be flattered when he is called a servant. Still there is no gainsaying that in answering the call to the ministry he is accepting a role as a humble servant of the Lord Jesus Christ. His very liberty derives from this servanthood. That he speaks for a God, *whose service is perfect freedom,* ought to compel him to consider well the relation between his service and his freedom.

I

Freedom derives from servanthood because people respect more the man who serves than the man who merely orates. The orator, indulging in grand verbal flourishes, may mightily impress an audience with his manner of speaking, but in what situation does the same audience listen to the same orator week after week and month after month? A man may be very easily admired as an orator without being respected as a person. The man who preaches enduringly has to have something more than verbal style. His preaching must come from an inner integrity which expresses itself in deeds of service.

The grandiloquence of the orator commands attention because it entertains. The power of the genuine preacher, on the other hand, gains respect because it edifies. The orator may be motivated by an ego "whose service is perfect thralldom," whereas the true preacher speaks in obedience to a God, "whose service is perfect freedom." People eventually weary of pure thralldom whereas they listen freely to the man who leads a life of service. The preacher need not be as flashy and fluent as the orator if the people who hear him know him as a servant of Christ. They will listen to him and permit him to speak freely because they respect him.

This is the paradox of Christian freedom which fascinated Martin Luther. In his famous *Treatise on Christian Liberty* Luther declared that "a Christian man is the most free lord of all, and subject to none; a Christian man is the most dutiful servant of all, and subject to everyone." The Christian man is so grateful for this spiritual freedom in Christ that he gladly serves his fellow man. That is exactly how the preacher feels who values his freedom in preaching Christ. This freedom is so precious to him that he expresses his gratitude for it through his service to his people. Hence he proclaims a God "whose service is perfect freedom." And his freedom is the greater and more meaningful simply because he offers himself as a servant. This is what Jesus told his disciples: "Whoever would be great among you must be your servant, and whoever would be first among you must be your slave" (Matt. 2:26, 27). It is therefore true, though paradoxically so, that the freedom of the pulpit depends on the slavery of the preacher!

Respect has to be based on something. In the case of a preacher it is granted, not because of the fluency and facility of his tongue, but by virtue of the services which proceed from his heart. This is at least the way I personally evaluate what a speaker has to say. There are certain speakers whose glibness and glamor cannot conceal their essential self-centeredness. They speak smoothly and volubly about the glories of the Christian life, but they command little respect when one knows they are more professionally than passionately devoted to the service thereof. One looks beneath the surface of words, probing for the evidence of deeds, not really hearing what a man is saying because what he *is* speaks so loudly.

Dr. Albert Schweitzer in his famous autobiography reveals a feeling which was a powerful factor in his decision to go to Africa as a medical missionary. He writes:

I wanted to be a doctor that I might be able to work without having to talk. For years I had been giving myself out in words and it was with joy that I had followed the calling of theological teacher and of preacher. But this new form of activity I could not represent to myself as being talking about the religion of love, but only as an actual putting it into practice. Medical knowledge made it possible for me to carry out my intention in the best and most complete way, wherever the path of service might lead me.[1]

There have been many times in my ministry when I have felt that I would be more persuasive in presenting the claims of the Christian life if I could only work without having to talk. Persons of multiple talents like Schweitzer are rare, but we who preach ought to be constantly aware of the words Paul wrote to the Corinthians: "For the kingdom of God does not consist in talk, but in power" (I Cor. 4:20). Surely the quality of a minister's service is an effective power which enables him to preach without having always to talk.

Recently I listened carefully for several days to a series of addresses by Clarence Jordan, founder and director of the Koinonia Farm in Georgia. He is a most eloquent and scholarly man who expounds the scriptures with an amplitude I have rarely heard. But he had my respect and sharply alerted attention before ever he opened his mouth because I knew what he had *done*. He was free to speak to me because I know something about his extraordinary witness for Christian race relations. That service made him free to say to me anything he chose because it was obviously

---

[1] *Out of My Life and Thought* (New York: Henry Holt and Co.).

based on courage, sacrifice, and accomplishment. This service had withstood the tests of boycott, violence, and isolation. My respect for him was boundless because his words were grounded in the most daring and dangerous service for Christ.

Likewise I find myself completely absorbed in the words of Norman Cousins, the distinguished editor of the *Saturday Review,* whenever I get to hear him speak. He, too, is free to speak to me because I know that he is so much more than a mere manipulator of words in his editorial columns. Underlying his powerful prose is the passionate commitment of a man to deeds of justice and mercy. In listening to him I cannot for a single moment forget his bold and imaginative leadership in helping to bring the Hiroshima Maidens of Japan to America for the surgical repair of physical disfigurements they suffered in history's first atomic destruction. I respect him the more because I know that he has given the same kind of leadership to the restoration of the Lapins of Poland who, as human guinea pigs, were the victims of Nazi bestiality.

When I first heard Martin Luther King, Jr., speak I sat in rapt and respectful attention because I knew that his world-wide fame was solidly based on his willingness to endure the extreme hazards of service to his people in Montgomery, Alabama. My estimation of this man was deepened when in his account of the Mongomery bus strike story in his book, *Stride Toward Freedom,* I read of his decision to go to Montgomery for his first pastorate rather than accept one of several more tempting offers in the North. He tells how he and his wife reached this decision:

For several days we talked and thought and prayed over each of these matters. Finally we agreed that, in spite of the disadvantages and inevitable sacrifices, our greatest service could be rendered in our native South. We came to the conclusion that we had something of a moral obligation to return —at least for a few years.

The South, after all, was our home. Despite its shortcomings we loved it as home, and had a real desire to do something about the problems that we had felt so keenly as youngsters. We never wanted to be considered detached spectators. Since racial discrimination was most intense in the South, we felt that some of the Negroes who had received a portion of their training in other sections of the country should return to share their broader contacts and educational experiences in its solution. Moreover, despite having to sacrifice much of the cultural life we loved, despite the existence of Jim Crow which kept reminding us at all times of the color of our skin, we had the feeling that something remarkable was unfolding in the South, and we wanted to be on hand to witness it.[2]

Surely Martin Luther King is a living witness to a God "whose service is perfect freedom." Could anyone doubt that the unusual effectiveness of his leadership of the fifty thousand Negro people of Montgomery was largely due to this willingness to serve? Throughout the long and exhausting months of the bus strike King preached to those people the hard gospel of love and nonviolent resistance. In perhaps the most incredible demonstration of the Christian ethic in American history they heard and heeded him because they knew they were being led by a servant of Jesus Christ. The freedom of the pulpit was *not* incidental to that moral and spiritual victory in Montgomery.

[2] (New York: Harper and Bros., 1958), pp. 21, 22.

II

This, then, suggests that the preacher's role as pastor is absolutely essential to his exercise of freedom in the pulpit. Pastoral experience is what truly fits a man to preach. It is both substance and freedom. *What* would he have to preach if he did not test the validity of the gospel in the crucibles of experience? And *where* would he get the freedom to preach if he were not willing to share in the trials and tribulations of his people? It is in his role as shepherd of the flock that the preacher acquires the dimension of freedom.

In the ever-increasing tendency of the ministry to imitate the highly-developed specializations of medicine and law, the minister who preaches is threatened with removal from reality. As our large churches grow larger, and our smaller ones smaller, church staffs seem to get divided into the ministry of the pulpit, the ministry of the parish, the ministry of education, the ministry of music, and so forth. This tends to perch the preacher on a lofty plane high above the experiences of the people, leaving the other specialists to know all about their weal and woe. Such a preacher reasons that it is his function to mount the holy stairs on Sunday and bedazzle the congregation with his brilliant speaking. Still, for all his brilliance, he can be stranger to his hearers if he has not served them in a personal way. Possibly he is threatened with something like the "space madness" which is going to be one of the greatest hazards of space travel. Engulfed in the vast voids of space our spacemen must contend with what is called sensory deprivation. This simply means cutting off the senses from familiar earth rhythms, sights, sounds, smells, and so on. Research has shown that man's ability to think properly deteriorates rapidly when he is subjected to prolonged sensory deprivation. Certainly the message of the preacher deteriorates when he subjects himself to prolonged disuse of his role as a pastor. He simply cuts himself off from the reality of the lives of his people and has little of any value or meaning to say to them.

Perhaps ministers lose something when they get "promoted" from their early pastorates where they functioned more literally as servants. As we move up the scale of pastoral appointments we like to think we have been liberated from the loathsome tasks of cranking out the weekly bulletins on the duplicating machine, mowing the church lawns, and firing the furnace when the janitor failed to show up. We say that all of this is a misuse of our time and training and maybe it is. But our willingness once to perform these duties with cheerfulness may have won us a precious freedom to preach which is not supplied by secretarial and janitorial staffs. The trouble is that there are so few vivid manifestations of our role as servants of the Lord.

I think of my own experience. In my first appointment out of seminary I got $250 added to my salary each year for serving as janitor. Now the rules of the game tell me that I don't have to do any of those things any more. From the position to which I have "progressed" I am now privileged to disdain such menial toil. But have I gained in the freedom to preach with moral and spiritual authority? In the spirit of the times most of our American churchmen are proud that their preachers' hands need no longer be soiled in common labor. But has the cleansing of our hands been at the expense of sealing our lips? Are our hands so antiseptic that our messages have become abstracted from real life?

All of this may sound hopelessly reactionary and unprogressive but I think we ought to remember that the lean and unlettered preachers of pioneer days on the American frontier exercised a freedom in their preaching which puts ours sometimes to shame. They believed with all of their hearts in a mighty God, in whose service they found perfect freedom. No pastoral duty was too mean for them. As I reflect on my own pastoral experience I believe I have been most free in the pulpit when I have been the best pastor to my people. Somehow it seems to me that there is a link between my freedom and the time when I helped tear up the church's old basement floor; when I helped move the furniture into the new building; when I have waited on tables at a church dinner; when I sat with a dying man throughout the night so that the family could rest; when I went to the hospital at three o'clock in the morning; when I flew a thousand miles in a single day to a distant city to see a man and wife who had been seriously injured in an auto accident; when I walked one evening through a long and dimly lighted underground passage to the hospital morgue with a grieving man to view the broken body of his wife, tragically struck down an hour before in an accident on the street. Yes, when a minister treads with his people the depths of life's despair, and when he walks with them along the summits of joy, he senses that as a pastor he is winning the right to preach with freedom. There is perfect freedom only in service.

E. Stanley Jones, a life-long missionary who understands that Christian missions these days must be based on Christian service, made a sage observation once when he said, "That man is not greatest who has the greatest number of servants, but that man is greatest who serves the largest number of people." In a day when the modern minister is directing more and more servants in both his house and his church he ought to ponder that. On the day the minister disdains his role as a pastor his freedom as a preacher shall cease. It is well to remember too that the apostle Paul, who plied his trade as a tentmaker throughout his unceasing missionary journeys, wrote to the church at Corinth: "For though I am free from all men, I have made myself a slave to all, that I might win the more" (I Cor. 9:19). That is a harsh and almost unacceptable word to the modern minister, but he ought to be reminded that as a pastor he is called to be a servant of all. In service is his freedom fulfilled.

III

It should be mentioned that a preacher enlarges the scope of his freedom when he devotes a portion of his ministry to the community at large. Certainly a minister ought to feel a responsibility for the welfare of the community which is much larger than the limits of his own parish. I will always be grateful for a dear lady in one of the churches I have served who one night in a board meeting stated that the church ought to expect its minister to participate in activities promoting the general welfare of the community. Some ministers seem to adopt a stance of virtue in withdrawing strictly into the work of their own parishes while declaring they haven't time for general community activities. I believe they sadly restrict their freedom because they thereby limit their service.

The minister who serves in programs of united fund raising for community welfare and on the boards of social agencies is demonstrating his desire to serve in the name of Christ. In these ways as in no others he is winning the respect of the community. Much of this kind of work is taxing and tiring but being a servant is never all fun. With many other ministers I have devoted countless hours to United Appeal and the work of the United Community Council. In this kind of work I have felt a deepening relationship with community leaders which gives me a greater freedom in taking my stand on the key issues of community life. I believe that by serving with them in the interests of the common welfare I win their respect, if not their agreement, on matters which I consider vital to the Christian witness. Without these opportunities for service I think I would have much less freedom. Participation in community activities enables a minister to witness to the God of his faith, "whose service is perfect freedom."

IV

The minister who seeks to be the servant of all builds a tolerance for his seeming arrogance when he preaches prophetically. When he is true to his calling the preacher would seem to conclude his pronouncements, as did the ancient prophets of Israel, with the assertion: "Thus saith the Lord." What sounds more arrogant and pretentious than *that?* Who is a mere mortal man to declare, "Thus saith the Lord"?

I can conceive of no other way for a mortal man to

preach in that way save he make himself the servant of all. Only when he fulfills himself as a servant of Christ will men permit him to make such an assertion. The beloved lines of Washington Gladden need to be the prayer evident on the lips of the preacher:

> O Master, let me walk with Thee
> In lowly paths of service free.

Only as a man walks in lowly paths of service is he truly free to speak for God. Otherwise men will be simply outraged by his pronouncements. The man who dares to speak for God must be humble before him, "whose service is perfect freedom."

As we read the New Testament it appears to us on our skeptical side that Jesus has made some arrogant, almost preposterous claims. Perhaps the doubter cannot be truly convinced until he comes to that place in the narrative when, as he was facing death upon the cross, Jesus rose from supper, laid aside his garments, and girded himself with a towel. Then pouring water into a basin, he began to wash the feet of his disciples, wiping them with the towel with which he was girded. It is this act of servanthood which helps us in the struggle with our unbelief. When a man serves like that his message cannot be easily repressed. Since preaching is an audacious and almost arrogant business we who engage in it ought to realize that we cannot be tolerated unless we speak out of lives of humble service. Preaching is pure foolishness unless we practice the service of Christ, which is perfect freedom.

Chapter VII

The Holy Compact Between Preacher and People

SEVERAL YEARS AGO IN CANTERBURY, ENGLAND, I saw this notice on a church door: "The Word of God will be preached in this Room on Lord's Day at 6:30 P.M.—God willing." Indeed God's word cannot be preached unless he is willing, but I do not think it is irreverent to suggest that the church must also be willing. Though God may endue his willing servants with the Holy Spirit and equip them eloquently to proclaim the gospel, if the people in the pews are not of a mind to listen, the word avails nothing.

Laymen have freedom too. The freedom of the pew is as essential and sacred as the freedom of the pulpit. If the preacher is free to speak the layman is free not to listen. In a strict sense the layman has the freedom to deny the pulpit's freedom by refusing to listen. What freedom has a preacher preaching to empty pews or inattentive heads? Moreover, in a democratically operated church lay officers are free to close their pulpit to whomever they disapprove. We need not cherish any romantic notion that every preacher is free to occupy any pulpit he chooses. Whatever freedom he has is a *grant*—at least in the Protestant sense —from his lay people. This freedom laymen can both give and take away. Earlier I have contended that a preacher's freedom is subject to certain limits and limitations. These, I said, he must accept. It ought to be recognized, especially by the preacher, that the layman in the pew also encounters limits, for, as a college dean said to me, "When the layman grants freedom to the preacher, he cuts down on his own freedom."

I have a deep conviction: wherever there is a great church distinguished for the freedom of its pulpit, there is a holy compact between preacher and people. In the terms of this compact the people guarantee the preacher the privilege of free utterance, and the preacher pledges himself, to them, to exercise this privilege, under God, with intelligence, responsibility, and honor. For a pulpit to be truly free preacher and people must believe in it with all of their Protestant passion.

The most brilliant example of this holy compact that I have ever known is to be seen in the First Methodist Church of Fvanston, Illinois. The pulpit of that church was made famous by the late Ernest Fremont Tittle. Dr. Tittle will always be for me a hero of the faith. Growing up in Illinois, I made frequent trips to hear him preach. I shall always remember his towering dignity, his profound thoughtfulness, his prophetic power. No pulpit was ever occupied by a freer man. But I am convinced that this demonstration of greatness cannot be finally accounted for save with reference to the valor and virtue of the lay leadership which granted that freedom and served as its ground. On not a few occasions Tittle's pronouncements aroused the wrath of certain groups in Chicago. Once when outside

forces sought to remove him from its leadership, the board
of that church issued a historic statement which said:

For some time a campaign of insinuation, misrepresentation
and slander, much of it anonymous, has been directed against
our pastor, Dr. Ernest F. Tittle. We believe that we owe it to
him and to our church, and to this community to assert un-
mistakenly our loyalty to him and our protest against such un-
American and unchristian procedure. . . .

We stand for a free pulpit and a free church. We do not
expect or desire a minister simply to echo the opinions of the
congregation, and we do not assert our individual agreement
with all of our minister's utterances. But we vigorously resent
the effort of outside organizations to dictate to the church or
to prescribe its message.[1]

Dr. Tittle was a great preacher but he would never have
been known as such had not the lay leaders of his church
lived up to the terms of the holy compact. That compact
was tested repeatedly in the crucible of fire, and both
preacher and people were faithful.

This holy compact is so vital to the meaning of Protes-
tantism that our churches ought to study its terms most
carefully. Implicit in it are these four essential considerations.

I

First, the degree to which a local church is able to furnish
and tolerate a free pulpit will depend basically on its concept of the ministry. The church must determine what it
expects its minister to be and do.

Perhaps most churches are confused between the proposi-

[1] *A Mighty Fortress* (New York: Harper and Bros.), p. xxiv.

tions that the minister is called by God, on the one hand, and by the congregation on the other. Frequently it appears that these are contradictory callings. The situation is familiar in which a congregation reacts against the message of its preacher when both they and he conceive of him as speaking for God. How can a congregation declare that some messages come through garbled while others are clear? Is the congregation a valid censor of the message, accepting and rejecting where it pleases? Fully recognizing that the minister is not an infallible spokesman for God, I would suggest that the church's concept of the ministry calls for the congregation to trust the personal integrity of its preacher. Ought not a church to issue a call to a man to assume its ministry because it believes he is called, not primarily by them, but by God? Would *they* want to call a man whom they believed *not* to be called by God? If they truly believe he is called by God, it would seem that they are morally and logically bound to grant him freedom to speak as God gives him light.

Malachi offered a definition of the priest which serves well as a model for the Protestant preacher: "For the lips of the priest should guard knowledge, and man should seek instruction from his mouth, for he is the messenger of the Lord of hosts" (2:7). One of the great Christian laymen of our time, former Congressman Brooks Hays of Arkansas, evidently holds this concept of the ministry. As violence broke out in Little Rock over desegregation in the public schools, and as conscientious ministers found themselves embroiled in conflicts with many of their parishioners, Hays declared that the minister must be allowed to speak as his conscience dictates. In the pulpit, said Hays, the minister is God's man, not the congregation's. Gerald W. Johnson, writing about "The Use and Abuse of Leadership," made a relevant observation which fits well into this concept of the ministry. "The leader," he wrote, "is necessarily one who breaks new paths into unfamiliar territory. The man who directs us along old ways is not a leader, he is a traffic cop—a useful and worthy functionary, but not inspiring." [2] Certainly Christian laymen who have studied the Old Testament prophets, and who know the significance of Jesus, can never conceive of the minister as a traffic cop.

Still it is difficult for laymen, in turbulent times, to accept the minister in the role of leader. A minister friend of mine told me recently of a most revealing evening he spent with a church-in-the-home group. Discussing the life of their church, several present voiced loud condemnation of preachers for not being more prophetic in the pulpit. The whole group seemed to agree that preachers should be more outspoken on key issues. Then my friend burst a bombshell, dramatically. He said to them: "Suppose your preacher next Sunday told you it was your Christian duty to sell your house to a Negro. Would you support him in this preachment?" At once the tenor and temper of the meeting changed. Almost everyone was outraged by this idea, declaring hotly that the preacher had no right to say that. Apparently the concept that the minister speaks for God is entertained in the abstract, but disapproved in the concrete. The injection of specificity is painful.

Does this mean that the congregation consists of puppets, sitting supinely in the pews, waiting to be manipulated

[2] *Saturday Review,* July 5, 1958, p. 30.

by the message of the preacher? At its deepest level the holy compact is much more than that. Bishop Francis J. McConnell set forth the real significance of this compact:

A congregation itself then may utter through the lips of a preacher a distinctive prophetic message. The preacher is to recognize this possibility and lift it to as high a level as may be. The initiative toward a larger message may indeed come from the mind of the congregation itself as the preacher learns that mind by intimate personal contact. The force in the message too may come from the congregation, but the preacher must strive to press into the wine of rare spiritual speech the best fruitage of the wisdom of his people.[3]

In the truly great church the preacher, as a servant of God, speaks on behalf of a people who have had the courage to hear and receive the gospel. In the words of P. T. Forsyth the minister is "to preach *to* the church *from* the Gospel so that with the church he may preach the Gospel to the world." Without the holy compact the gospel could not reach into the world. The laity must not see the freedom of the pulpit as existing in a vacuum. It does in fact exist in the context of their faith. By making the pulpit truly free, laymen exalt and participate in the preaching of the gospel. They must know, where this is true, that it is they who build and guard the channels through which the word of God may freely flow.

The British Methodists have a beautiful custom which illustrates this concept of the ministry. Just before the minister enters the pulpit to open the worship, the stewards

[3] *The Preacher and the People* (New York: The Abingdon Press, 1922), pp. 108-9.

meet with him in the vestry. There they help him into his robe and in a most solemn and expectant moment one of them prays that God on that day will enable his servant to preach truly the word of God. Then as the minister goes to the pulpit, and they to their pews, they know that they have helped to prepare the way for what they shall hear.

II

Second, there is the debatable question as to whether this holy compact warrants personal and private relationships between the minister and individual members of his congregation. I have close friends who are profoundly convinced that the minister should not mix too intimately, in a social and personal sense, with members of his congregation. They sincerely believe that such relationships limit the preacher's freedom to speak forthrightly on vital issues. They believe that familiarity breeds contempt, and control. Is the holy compact better served by the minister standing at a safe and prudent distance from his people?

Obviously the minister's own personal propensities must largely determine the answer. Ministers do not all have the same personality. I respect my friends whose own traits fit them more readily into a professional-type relationship. I recognize the hazards of my own approach, but I should have to confess that my own personal needs cause me to seek intimate friendships among my people. I do not feel that relating closely to my people has ever muted my message in the pulpit. I am unaware of any necessity to "take it easy" on any of my friends when preparing a sermon. Real friendship, I believe, is something vastly different from "cronyism." True friends respect each other and expect to differ. When friendships are based on Christian love friends can disagree. Certainly a real friend will respect one's professional function, just as one enjoying intimate friendship with a physician would expect that physician to tell him the truth about his state of health if his professional judgment were sought. Naturally this is the kind of friendship I believe a minister can have with his laymen.

There is an amazing relevance to this discussion in the original meaning of the word "freedom." Though from the Old English, it is related to the Old Norse term meaning love and peace, possibly, as Wilfred Funk points out, "because peace and love are at their best when people are free." Thus real freedom grows out of love, and a loving friend would never regard another as a slave. This is relevant because it seems to me that it is exactly the kind of relationship the minister ought to ripen with his people. Where there is a relationship of real friendship the minister will be free.

Though I would not cavalierly brush aside the wise counsel of those who do not share this view, I do believe that the holy compact between preacher and people can be deepened and secured when the preacher enters into real friendship with his people.

III

Third, the holy compact is a two-way street. It enjoins the preacher to respect the freedom of his parishioners to reject his views. It does not give him the right to regard himself as an unanswerable oracle.

Here is a cardinal consideration for the preacher as a

Protestant. The right of private judgment is a principle distinguishing the Protestant faith. It is a right not reserved exclusively for the preacher. It belongs as well to laymen. Many preachers, tending to pontificate, forget that Protestant laymen may only be persuaded, not coerced. Freedom, in the Protestant sense, does not mean the absence of conflict. Conflicting views are neither foreign nor unhealthful in the Protestant church. The preacher must expect that his laymen will subject his ideas to the scrutiny of their own private judgment. Indeed, if he is a true Protestant, he will invite them to do this. No attitude or pose of his ought even to hint that he regards himself as being above criticism. He must not be offended to learn that "roast preacher" is served on Sunday in the homes of his congregation. Indeed the holy compact of which I speak will achieve a high purpose if he has sufficient rapport with his people to be invited by them to share, at leisure, in a "feast of ideas."

Actually this is simply a way of giving further substantiation to the idea that a minister attains a maximum effectiveness in his ministry when he knows his people as friends. For, as one thoughtful layman said to me, if the minister wants to be friendly with his people he must expect those who are true friends to judge him just as he judges them. Hence the freedom of the pulpit has a bulwark, never failing.

IV

Fourth, in analyzing the terms of this holy compact I think laymen will agree that to deny the freedom of pulpit is to sentence the preacher to mediocrity. Though freedom does not in itself guarantee excellence, I am certain that its denial so devitalizes any preacher that he cannot arise above the dull and drab. This condition, I submit, a congregation will find unacceptable because it is unendurable.

The preacher whose thoughts and utterances are strictly controlled by the congregation is a preacher condemned—certainly with his consent—to mediocrity. No one in the pews can long respect a preacher who lacks conviction. Conviction is an enlivening and energizing force in the sermon. The man whose convictions can be curbed soon drifts into the sluggish state of a drone. Being tedious and trying, no congregation can endure him for long. There is a cost to the control of the pulpit: it is boredom. Sermons prerecorded by the congregation and mechanically transscribed on the tongue of a preacher, are so obviously "phony" that even those who record them in the first place can hardly bear to listen.

The congregation which resents mediocrity profoundly would do what I heard suggested by Harvey J. D. Seifert: "We ought to go to the bishop when we have a preacher who Sunday after Sunday says nothing but that with which we already agree." The self-respecting church, with standards of excellence, would be then honoring its part of the holy compact. No congregation can for long suffer the preacher whom it can throttle. Monitoring of the pulpit makes for mediocrity.

Perhaps no one in American history has more amply and articulately proclaimed the freedom of the pulpit than Stephen S. Wise, the great rabbi and founder of the Free Synagogue in New York City. I have referred to him repeatedly because his works and words abound with this concern. In his autobiography he recounts the celebrated incident when, as a young rabbi in Oregon, he was invited to preach a series of trial sermons at Temple Emanu-El of New York, known as the Cathedral Synagogue of America. When the controlling interests of that institution made it clear that "the pulpit shall always be subject to, and under the control of, the board of trustees," Rabbi Wise refused to be considered further for the call. The open letter he wrote in explanation of this action and defense of the idea of a free pulpit, ought to be read by every Protestant layman and minister who cherishes the freedom of his heritage. In it are these words:

> The chief office of the minister, I take it, is not to represent the views of the congregation, but to proclaim the truth as he sees it. How can he serve a congregation as a teacher save as he quickens the minds of his hearers by the vitality and independence of his utterances? But how can a man be vital and independent and helpful, if he be tethered and muzzled? A free pulpit, worthily filled, must command respect and influence; a pulpit that is not free, howsoever filled, is sure to be without potency and honor.[4]

And I would ask, how can a preacher quicken the minds of his hearers, how can he be potent and honorable, how can he avoid mediocrity, if he is not free?

The willingness of laymen to enter this holy compact has had special meaning for me. In Indianola Church I have stood in a pulpit whose freedom has been vigorously

[4] *Challenging Years* (New York: G. P. Putnam's Sons, 1949), p. 91.

and valiantly guarded by great laymen for over fifty years. One day, many years ago, Robert Leonard Tucker, a predecessor, condemned from the pulpit the political practices of the governor of the State of Ohio. Following the service a group of five lawyers waited upon him when the church had emptied. They informed him that he was going to be in serious trouble because of that pronouncement. They gave it as their professional opinion that on the morrow he would be sued. Then they walked out of the church and left the young preacher shivering with apprehension. In a few minutes, however, they returned—all five of them. Their spokesman said: "Tucker, we want you to know that we still think you are in trouble. But we also want you to know that we will defend you." And to this day Indianola Church has a free pulpit because there are still laymen who honor this sacred pact.

Chapter VIII

The Transforming Power of Grace

IN HIS *Recollections,* WASHINGTON GLADDEN RE-
marked that he could see no other place of influence in the
world in which a man can be as free as in the Christian
pulpit. Realizing that some preachers habitually wear the
halters of cowardice and subserviency, he believed nonetheless that the minister has more freedom in speaking his
mind than most moral teachers.

I have been saying things, with no sense of restraint, during
the last fifty years, that I should not have been so likely to
say if I had been a journalist or a college professor. I have
not always commanded the assent of all my auditors, but they
have recognized my right to speak, and have never sought to
muzzle me. I doubt if any other kind of work, in which a
living was to be made, would have given me so large an opportunity as my churches in North Adams and Springfield and
Columbus have given me to speak my deepest thought.[1]

Despite the many incursions against the freedom of the
pulpit which exist today—and which have always existed
—I share Gladden's faith. Seeking seriously to be "a work-
man who has no need to be ashamed, rightly handling the
word of truth," (II Tim. 2:15) a minister will find him-

[1] (Boston: Houghton Mifflin Co., 1909), p. 416.

self committed to the freest of all professions. The professions of law, medicine, and teaching all have their glorious freedoms, but none is as finally free as the preacher in the pulpit. Though this may appear to be a cause of pride and exultation, it is certainly, when more profoundly understood, to be soberly accepted as an unmerited gift. Not only is it a gift, but an awesome responsibility, for, as Paul confessed, "if I preach the gospel, that gives me no ground for boasting. *For necessity is laid upon me.* Woe to me if I do not preach the gospel!" (I Cor. 9:16.) The preacher is free only because of a most peculiar and precious gift. It is not the gift of his own intellectual acumen, or his own native courage, or his human ability to love, or the forbearance of his laymen. That which makes him free is the sheer gift of God's grace.

No real preacher would dare to believe that either his freedom or his effectiveness is due to his own talents and merits. If he truly preaches the gospel he knows that he is under the absolute necessity of beseeching God for the outpouring of his grace. He needs that grace for two reasons: first, preaching is a daring, almost arrogant, certainly a presumptuous act. May a man pretend to speak for God? How could he dare open his mouth without calling upon the grace of God? And second, preaching is a *man* speaking to *men* the gospel which is a scandal unto the world. What is to prevent his courage from crumbling as he proclaims what people do not really want to hear, save the grace of God? Grace is required in every profession, but, by its very nature, immeasurably more in the ministry.

If the God whom we preach is so much greater than the jukebox images of "He!" and "The Man Upstairs," if

God has created a world of incredible vastness and unfathomable mystery, if he dwells in light unapproachable, may a man stand in a pulpit and claim to be his spokesman? Did the ancient prophet hear God aright?

> For my thoughts are not your thoughts,
>   neither are your ways my ways, says the Lord.
> For as the heavens are higher than the earth,
>   so are my ways higher than your ways
>   and my thoughts than your thoughts.
>   (Isa. 55:8, 9)

What an impertinence of the preacher it is to speak words for God! How can his words have meaning when his thoughts are not God's thoughts? What thoughts does he have to distinguish the words he claims to speak for God from the words men speak to him? What else is there to say except that when a man dares to speak the word of God, in his own words, he must first tremble and be transformed by the power of grace? He must learn to place himself in the hands of God, and he must know that "it is a fearful thing to fall into the hands of the living God."

In the first chapter I sought to point out how badly preaching is crippled by acquiescence to the spirit of the times. Just as the atmosphere of the earth obscures our view of the limitless wonders of the universe, so do the frailties of the minister obstruct his vision of God. Striving always to bring the truth of God into sharper focus, he must honestly conclude. "For now we see in a mirror dimly." The limits and limitations of the preacher loom in the foreground of every sermon. Never can the realistic preacher take his place in the pulpit without fervently praying, as did the ancient psalmist, "O Lord, open thou my lips, and my mouth shall show forth thy praise" (Ps. 51:15). He knows that he cannot *show forth* the glory of God until, by grace, God removes the dissension from his soul.

It takes a great deal of grace, for example, for the preacher to maintain a healthy realism about himself. Often the object of undue adulation and praise, he needs to beware of the temptations to pride. Just because he has responded to a holy calling does not certify him as a saint. He must know deep within his heart that he can never measure up to the somewhat romantic image his people have of him. Praise is a heady wine, and the well-received preacher may drink too deeply of it. It is so easy to mistake rhetorical talent for spiritual virtue. It is gratifying to look down upon a congregation and feel them eating from your hand. In such a moment of satisfaction it is difficult to distinguish between cleverness of speech and profundity of content. Truly the head of many a preacher has been "turned" by what the congregation might applaud as success.

In an expansive mood a man may say, "I just love to preach!" Certainly no one can complain of a man's love for his work, but this is an exultation which ought to be subjected to the most searching self-criticism. Does he love to preach because he loves God or because he loves the sound of his own voice? Does the power of God flow through his preaching, sometimes bringing him agony of soul, or does he love the power over people that preaching gives? Though the freest of all professions, the ministry by its very nature is also perilously mined with a thousand appealing decoys. The minister exercises his great freedom only as he calls upon the grace of God to enable him to detect and avoid the seductions which lie deceivingly on the surfaces over which he must daily move. His need for grace must be deeply and desperately felt. He must join Paul in saying: "Not that we are sufficient of ourselves to claim anything as coming from us; our sufficiency is from God, who has qualified us to be ministers of a new covenant" (II Cor. 3:5-6*a*).

Where will the preacher find this grace? How will it be given to him? The source of grace, and hence of freedom, is identified in the insight of Paul when he wrote to the Corinthians, "Now the Lord is the Spirit, and where the Spirit of the Lord is, there is freedom" (II Cor. 3:17). The preacher is transformed by the power of grace and delivered into freedom when he seeks first in his life to entertain the Spirit of the Lord. Freedom is preserved, not because he is good or wise or eloquent, but because the Spirit working in him wages victorious warfare against the ravages of deceit and decay.

George A. Gordon has helped us to understand the content of this grace by relating the question of freedom to the question of good. He wrote in his autobiography:

Experience teaches man what appears to be good and is not, and what is real, essential, changeless good. The will of man guided by the natural good comes under its sovereignty; and here it must be said that apart from good freedom has no meaning. To be forever under the sway of the greatest good is to be perfect in freedom. The will, good, real and unreal, and freedom belong together; they constitute the field in which our moral life grows." [2]

The Christian, of course, finds this sovereign good in the person of Christ. Life in Christ constitutes "the field in which our moral life grows." Where does the Christian preacher obtain grace? Indeed he will find it alone in Jesus Christ. Gordon also declared that "The Christian pulpit is the creation of Christ, and its power will last only so long as his spirit controls and inspires it." [3] Moreover, he suggests that "As a preliminary in the discussion of the place of Christ in the pulpit of today, it must be remarked that preachers need to revive the sense of the supremacy of their calling by living more completely under the shadow of the Divine Preacher." It seems clear to me that we preachers will never revive the sense of the supremacy of our calling until we learn to derive the fulfillment of our two greatest needs—freedom and grace—from him who is full of grace and truth. We must perceive with the author of Ephesians, "Of this gospel I was made a minister according to the gift of God's grace which was given me by the working of his power" (3:7).

Franklin D. Elmer, Jr., has put in words, which I greatly cherish, a description of the preacher recognizing his calling, his fragility, his awful need for the presence of Christ:

> He stands between the ever
> And the now—
> A slender, tender,
> Fragile coupling.

[2] *My Education and Religion*, p. 243.
[3] *The Christ of Today*, p. 251.

The Transforming Power of Grace

Through him pass the yearnings
Of the bruised and battered
Sons of earth—
The fervid hopes and prayers
Of cosmic neophytes
Perplexed and lost and lonely,
Clamoring for comfort
And hungering for courage
In communion with the soul of souls.

Through him comes, returning,
That strange mysterious flood
Of power—
The stream of hope and healing,
The word of everlasting wisdom,
The hand outstretched. . . .

And there is none but Christ
With whom to share his anguish
As he finds himself
Too slender
Too tender
Too fragile.[4]

This "Too slender, too tender, too fragile" preacher experiences an existential moment when he takes his place in the pulpit. On his human side, and understanding the nature of the gospel he is about to proclaim, he knows that he stands absolutely alone. Trembling in every limb he knows that "it is a fearful thing to fall into the hands of the living God." Hence he implores Almighty God for grace. Then, if he truly preaches, a divine metamorphosis occurs. What he has prepared by the sweat of his brow be-

[4] *Christian Century*, August 12, 1953, p. 913. Used by permission.

comes something other than his own. His words bear the awful weight of the word of God. Now he knows what Paul meant when he said: *"For necessity is laid upon me.* Woe to me if I do not preach the gospel!" And still from across the centuries come the words: "You will know the truth, and the truth will make you free." Since that truth is really Jesus Christ, the preacher knows what makes and keeps his pulpit free.